CW01604655

Stand and Deliver!

ISBN: 9781864765 076

Copyright © Axiom Publishing, 2007.
Unit 2, 1 Union Street, Stepney, South Australia, 5069.

This book is copyright. Apart from any fair dealing for the purpose of private study, research, criticism or review, as permitted under the Copyright Act, no part may be reproduced by any process without written permission. Enquiries should be made to the publisher.

Axiom Australia
www.axiompublishing.com.au

Printed in Malaysia

Stand and Deliver!

By Michelle O'Regan

Contents

Foreword

"Stand and deliver!"

Some would consider the call to stand and deliver a toast or speech as daring a proposition as a duel by dawn light, pistols at twenty paces! In fact, it's often said that people fear speaking in public more than death: all the more reason to work through this unreasoned terror. Face your fear and do it anyway!

The formula is incredibly simple:

Stand up! Speak up! Then, shut up and sit Down!

Seriously, with some pointers on preparation and delivery, you will soon find yourself looking forward to speaking opportunities.

Three simple things underpin any effective speech, be it long or short:

Heart —speaking from the heart with sincerity is key to effective speaking. 'They may not remember what you said, but they will always remember the way you made them feel'. When you speak from the heart it goes straight to the hearts of your audience — you gain rapport and empathy.

Humour — sprinkled not added. It must feel right for you, not forced…as right as the jacket or shoe that fits well. A self-deprecating anecdote about one's work life delivered during a retirement or resignation speech where you are prepared to make yourself the subject of humour or a quote or joke you feel quite at home delivering are excellent vehicles. To begin with humour is a great way of disarming your audience.

Humility—being humble is as good a guiding principle whilst on your feet delivering a speech, as it is in life. Remembering the purpose of delivering the toast or speech will keep the speaker humble—the toast is meant to spotlight the person or people one is toasting, not the speaker. The speech is delivered to convey information, to give thanks or to show appreciation and this applies in acceptance and retirement speeches as well.

Being mindful of remaining humble also keeps the nerves at bay. When it's not about you—them looking at you and judging you—speaking can become the pleasure that it is because it has shifted the focus to the people we address and our intention to convey good will or knowledge or fellow feeling.

Stand and Deliver! provides helpful tips, formulas and guides for speeches and toasts with quotes suited to life's occasions.

So here's a toast to you, the speech and toast giver:

May speaking become you more each day
Finding the words your intent to convey
Keeping it simple, going straight to the heart
Lifting the spirit, good will to impart.

The Art of Speech Making

Speech Alive!

Do you want your speech to be memorable? Would you like to reach out to the audience with your words? Here are some aspects which will really help in preparation and delivery.

Words Said, Not Read

You are preparing a speech for an audience who cannot listen at their own pace, who cannot ask you to repeat something unclear, and are unable to have input into the way you have ordered your ideas.

As a speechwriter, you need to think like a listener and write like a talker. The trick is to speak the words out loud before you write them down. Each element, each sentence, each paragraph will be built from what has gone before: moving from the general to the specific, from the known to the unknown and from the present to the future.

Paint A Sensory Picture With Your Language

Using word pictures allows the audience to engage their imaginations. Instead of saying, for instance, that a meal was delicious, use adjectives and specifics which will conjure up sights, smells and tastes. Use imagery to bring your anecdotes to life. If the groom, for example, speaks of the first time he met his new bride, what she wore, where they were, the sense impressions that made it memorable, this is powerful communication as it has involved the listeners and allows them to experience the tale.

Keep It Moving Along

Having scripted some funny or moving stories, the next challenge is to weave them together to form a whole. From beginning to end, your presentation should flow smoothly and seamlessly.

There are some simple ways to change tack or direction —"meanwhile", "however" and "but" are bridging words; rhetorical questions are another method of moving from one direction to another. You've spoken about the past, "Now what advice can I offer for their future?" Physical movement can change emphasis or focus, turning the eyes or the body in the direction you want to speak. Pause is also useful is notifying the listeners that you might have finished, before you begin again and move into some other area.

Three Attention Grabbers

Use Humour To Disarm And Relax Them

Examples:

Ladies and gentlemen, the last time I gave a speech, someone shouted from the back "I can't hear you!" The man sitting beside me said, "Let's trade places!"

Ladies and gentlemen, the toastmaster just asked me, "Would you like to speak now or should we let our guests enjoy themselves just a little while longer?"

Ladies and gentlemen, before I start speaking I have something to say.

Use A Quotation To Get Their Attention

Examples:

Ladies and gentlemen, here is Ogden Nash's secret to a happy union: " when you're wrong, admit it, when you're right, shut up!"

Ladies and gentlemen, Mr Anonymous wrote this piece of wisdom, "Marriage is a mutual partnership when both parties know when to be mute."

Quote 'On This Day'

Open by telling your audience the significance of this day in history which dovetails with this event. It is a good idea to triangulate with a famous birth and a landmark occasion. Details can be found on website www.OnThisDay.com

Examples:

Ladies and gentlemen, this day is steeped in significance. This day, the 7th of July was the day of Beatle drummer Ringo Starr's birth, in 1940; and in 1988, the live Aid concerts were held in London and Philadelphia raising millions for famine relief. And on this day 200X, James married Pamela.

Tips For Speaking Well

Speed

Time yourself delivering the speech, bearing in mind that you will be speaking more slowly than you normally would—you need to factor in opportunities for audience response and pause.

Aim for 100 words per minute (wpm) when you are rehearsing —this usually transfers to about 130 wpm when you are actually speaking. The word count to aim for in a five-minute delivery is 600 wpm.

Pause

Pauses are the most natural way to give emphasis and structure to your words and sentences. Pauses can build for dramatic effect, allowing anticipation to mount.

They can be used in different ways:

- Before a key phrase or sentence
- Between a change in mood, moving from a lighthearted moment to something more serious
- Mid sentence, for dramatic effect or to deliver a punch line
- Before your conclusion
- Before your toast.

Articulation

This means being able to speak clearly. Were your words clear? Were your words distinct from each other? Did you hear the ends of your sentences, or did they fall away?

Here are a few ways you can improve your diction:

- Place more emphasis on the consonants.

- Move your lips more than you normally would.
- Try leaving a small pause between each word.

Emphasis

In order to make your delivery a winning one, you need to place meaningful emphasis on the key words, phrases and syllables. Remember the audience is hearing this for the first and last time, so you need to help them make meaning of your message. Changing emphasis can change meaning, so check yourself to make sure you have the emphasis on the right terms. If you are using cue cards, underline the key phrases or syllables to provide prompts.

Pronunciation

Are the words you have chosen easy for you to pronounce? If there are some you have difficulty with, this may confuse your audience. Choose substitutes, ones you can pronounce.

Projection

Will everyone in the room be able to hear you? If you have doubts, you may need to work on projection.

Here are some tips that should help.

- Open your mouth more than you would normally when speaking.
- Hold your head up.
- Speak more slowly than you would normally.

Whole-Body Communication

Your audience does much more than just listen to your speech —they experience it. The way you deliver your speech is as important as the words you choose. Here are some tips which will help you project positivity and sincerity.

The Proper Stance

Stand upright with your feet shoulder width apart and just slightly turned out. This means you can move your weight from one foot to the other without it being noticed. Stand well away from the table. Leaning on the table can give out a message of aggression, or else you could spill more than the contents of your glass. Keep your hands out of your pockets and refrain from grasping them to the front or back. If you have cue cards, hold them in one palm or place them on the table in plain sight so you can refer to them when you choose. Resist the temptation to shield yourself, even if it's just with your arms. This gives your audience the message that you are being defensive. Not shielding gives the unspoken message that you are open and friendly.

Reinforcing Your Verbal Communication

When it comes to delivering your speech, there are two extremes, neither of which you want to emulate. One is delivering your speech in such a stiff unmoving way that you resemble a wax effigy. The other is waving your arms around like a human windmill. You can make simple hand gestures, which reinforce your words without distracting your audience.

Hostile vs Friendly

Crossed arms are seen as negative and defensive. Open arms and open palms are on the other hand perceived as friendly and open.

Hands and fingers pointing upwards or finger-wagging are perceived as hostile gestures, whereas open palms with fingers pointing downwards are seen as friendly and non-threatening.

Bad Habits

Be aware of any bad habits you might have—do any of these apply to you?

- Swaying
- Shuffling your feet
- Rustling notes
- Talking with your hand in front of your mouth
- Jingling coins in your pocket
- Excessive waving of hands.

The ideal way to pick up on these bad habits is to take a video of yourself whilst speaking; if you don't have a video, deliver a rehearsal of your speech in front of a friend or family member you trust to give you honest feedback.

Eye Contact

There's a special technique that professional speakers use—it's called the *lighthouse technique*, which means beaming all around the room slowly, tracing the X or Z shape continually but varying the size and shape each time. This prevents your eye contact from being noticeable and predictable.

It's okay to stop just long enough on one individual to give them the impression the speech is intended for them alone, but not so long that it seems you've singled them out.

Smiling

When it's a celebratory or congratulatory event, there is nothing more engaging than a smile. It exudes warmth, it's an unspoken way of saying you are very happy to be here, that you just know everyone is going to have a great time, and it spreads smiles contagiously across the room.

In Summary

The goal is to captivate the audience, and this will depend largely on what you project. You are aiming for confidence, sincerity and rapport. Be aware of how you come over by working on these:

- A sincere wish to communicate
- Striking a conversational approach
- Upright posture and open stance
- Apt movements and fluid gestures
- Lively eyes and facial expressions
- An expressive voice.

Acceptance speeches

Sooner or later—especially if you are involved in achievement, leadership or philanthropy—you're going to receive an award and be called upon to say something. Regard this as a marvellous opportunity to give back to the organisation you have spent your time and efforts on, which has engaged your energy and interest. Your peers have judged you deserving.

Acceptance, appreciation and awe—be grateful, gracious and humble— but not so self-effacing that you appear to be trivialising this honour.

Whenever you are given advance notice, make sure you ask how long you are expected to speak. The shorter the speech, the more practice you will need. When the moment comes, connect with your audience.

General guides

Keep it brief

Even if you've been notified in advance that you will receive an award or acknowledgment, practice keeping it tight and to the point.

Jane Fonda, Best Actress for *Klute,* kept it very short and memorable: "There's a great deal to say, but I'm not going to say it tonight." (1972)

Keep the politics out

This occasion should not be used as the soapbox for personal opinions. This is about the audience and the occasion.

Make it memorable

You can do precisely that by saying something that distills your uniqueness and appreciation.

Touch people's hearts

Showing genuine emotion forms a bridge of connection to others, which is very powerful. Halle Berry, recipient of the Best Actress Award for 2001, was in tears when she spoke "This moment…is for the women that stand beside me and for every nameless, faceless woman of colour that now has a chance because the door tonight has been opened."

Be gracious

Meryl Streep was extremely gracious when accepting her Best Actress award for *Sophie's Choice* in 1981, "I have a lot of people to thank and I'm going to be one of those people that tries to mention a lot of names, because I know just two seconds ago my mother and father went berserk and I'd like to give some other mothers and fathers that same opportunity."

Thank you

There is nothing more powerful than heartfelt thanks. Harrison Ford received the Cecil B DeMille Award in 2002 and his words were classic: "I wrote two speeches, a long one and a short one. I'll give you the short one. 'Thank you.' But it seems that there might be enough time for the long one as well, which is: 'Thank you very much.'"

Don't read from notes – preferable to waffling, or wandering of course

It's a real dampener when someone pulls out a piece of paper (unless of course that's part of a gag where you summarily rip it up or let it fall, explaining that you had a whole speech prepared but...if you do need prompts, by all means use keywords written on cards that can be held in the palm of your hand.

Don't apologise / don't be negative

Be upbeat not downbeat, unless you are quite as accomplished as someone like Woody Allen who makes depression seem quite hilarious.

Excerpts from famous acceptance speeches

William Faulkner's acceptance speech for the Nobel Prize for Literature 1950

Faulkner had avoided speaking publicly his entire writing career so there was a great deal of interest in what he would say when he travelled to Stockholm to receive the prize.

" I feel that this award was not made to me as a man, but to my work—a life's work in the agony and sweat of the human spirit, not for glory and least of all for profit, but to create out of the materials of the human spirit something which did not exist before. So this award is only mine in trust.

"...the young man or woman writing today has forgotten the problems of the human heart in conflict with itself which alone can make good writing because only that is worth writing about, worth the agony and the sweat. He must learn them again. He must teach himself that the basest of all things is to be afraid: and, teaching himself that, forget it forever, leaving no room in his workshop for anything but the old verities and truths of the heart, the universal truths lacking which any story is ephemeral and doomed—love and honour and pity and pride and compassion and sacrifice."

Martin Luther King's Acceptance Speech for Nobel Prize for Peace 1964, excerpt

"I accept this award today with an abiding faith in America and an audacious faith in the future of mankind. I refuse to accept despair as the final response to the ambiguities of history. I refuse to accept the idea that the 'isness' of man's present nature makes him morally incapable of reaching up for the eternal 'oughtness' that forever confronts him.

"I refuse to accept the idea that man is mere flotsom and jetsom in the river of life unable to influence the unfolding events which surround him. I refuse to accept the view that mankind is so tragically bound to the starless midnight of racism and war that the bright daybreak of peace and brotherhood can never become a reality.

I refuse to accept the cynical notion that nation after nation must spiral down a militaristic stairway into the hell of thermonuclear destruction. I believe that unarmed truth and unconditional love will have the final word in reality. This is why right temporarily defeated is stronger than evil triumphant."

John Steinbeck (excerpt), Acceptance Speech Nobel Prize for Literature 1962

"Literature is as old as speech. It grew out of human need for it and it has not changed except to become more needed. The skalds, the bards, the writers are not separate and exclusive. From the beginning, their functions, their duties, their responsibilities have been decreed by our species...the writer is delegated to declare and to celebrate man's proven capacity for greatness of heart and spirit—for gallantry in defeat, for courage, compassion and love. In the endless war against weakness and despair, these are the bright rally flags of hope and of emulation. I hold that a writer who does not passionately believe in the perfectibility of man has no dedication nor any membership in literature."

Memorable acceptance quotes

Hattie McDaniel, Mammy in *Gone with the Wind*, best supporting actress (first black performer to win an Oscar)
"This is one of the happiest moments of my life, and I want to thank each one of you who had a part in selecting for one of the awards, for your kindness. It has made me feel very, very humble; and I shall always hold it as a beacon for anything that I may be able to do in the future. I sincerely hope I shall always be a credit to my race and to the motion picture industry. My heart is too full to tell you just how I feel, and may I say thank you and God bless you."

Jack Benny, accepting an award
"I really don't deserve this. But I have arthritis and I don't deserve that either."

Grace Kelly, 1954 Academy Awards
"This is one night I wish I smoked and drank."

Louise Fletcher (Nurse Ratchett), 1976 Academy Awards
"I'd like to thank Jack Nicholson for making being in a mental institution like being in a mental institution. I loved being hated by you."

Cate Blanchett, Best Supporting Actress (playing the part of Katharine Hepburn), *The Aviator*
"I don't have a sense of entitlement or that I deserve this. You'd be surprised at the lack of competition between nominees—I think a lot of it's imposed from the outside. Can I have my champagne now?"

Kim Basinger, 1998 Academy Awards
"I just want to thank everybody I've ever met in my entire life."

Robin Williams, *Good Will Hunting*
"Most of all, I want to thank my father, up there, the man who when I said I wanted to be an actor, he said, 'Wonderful. Just have a back-up profession like welding'."

Whoopi Goldberg, 1991 Academy Awards
"As a little kid, I lived in the projects and you're the people I watched. You're the people who made me want to be an actor. I'm so proud to be here."

Reese Witherspoon, *Walk the Line*, 2006
"I am so blessed to have my family here tonight. My mother and my father are here. And I just want to say thank you so much for everything, for being so proud of me. It didn't matter if I was making my bed or making a movie. They never hesitated to say how proud they were of me. And that means so very much to a child. So thank you, Mom and Dad. I want to say thank you to my wonderful husband and my two children who should be going to bed. And thank you for loving me so much and supporting me."

Anniversaries

If you are called upon to deliver a speech for your parents or special friends who are celebrating a landmark-wedding anniversary, there are several ways to structure the material.

Arriving at a theme is essential. Think about just a few qualities of the relationship that stand out, and then reflect on stories or anecdotes which demonstrate these characteristics.

Another approach is to place their wedding date in a social history context.

"Twenty years ago on this day, the Berlin Wall came down, peace was declared in BXXXXX, and Robert married Alice in a tiny little church in Mudgereeba and they made a home for themselves at 210 Balboa Road, Bundi."

Alternately, chronicle the path these two have taken and the challenges they have faced.

"Little did these two know when they said "I do", on xxx (date) what they were agreeing to. Little did they know that in a matter of a decade they would be parents to no less than YYY children, that they would have moved home and country ZZZ times...etc."

Weaving a quote into your speech is also a great starting point, and may form a pivot for your theme.

LBJ was famous for a few things. One was his "peace salute" and the other was the secret of his long marriage to Lady Bird: "I have learned that only two things are necessary to keep one's wife happy. First, let her think she's having her own way. And second, let her have it."...

"When I asked Ted what he thought the secret of their long happy marriage was, he said: 'We never go to bed angry. We stay up and fight.' But seriously..."

Anniversary quotes

"There is nothing nobler or more admirable than when two people who see eye to eye keep house as man and wife, confounding their enemies and delighting their friends."
—Homer, Odyssey, ninth century B.C.

"An archaeologist is the best husband any woman can have; the older she gets, the more interested he is in her."
—Agatha Christie

Albert Einstein, on his fiftieth wedding anniversary:

"When we first got married, we made a pact. It was this: in our life together, it was decided I would make all of the big decisions and my wife would make all the little decisions. For fifty years, we have held true to this agreement. I believe that this is the reason for the success of our marriage. However, the strange thing is that in fifty years, there hasn't been one big decision."

"My parents stayed together for forty years, but that was out of spite."
—Woody Allen

"We are all a little weird and life's a little weird, and when we find someone whose weirdness is compatible with ours, we join up with them and fall in mutual weirdness and call it love."

—Author Unknown

"Our wedding was many years ago.
The celebration continues to this day."
—Gene Perret

"It's easy to understand love at first sight, but how do we explain love after two people have been looking at each other for years?"
—Author Unknown

"A good marriage is like a casserole, only those responsible for it really know what goes in it."—Anonymous

"The sum which two married people owe to one another defies calculation. It is an infinite debt, which can only be discharged through eternity."
—Johann Wolfgang von Goethe

"Don't marry the person you think you can live with;
marry only the individual you think
you can't live without."
—Dr. James C. Dobson

"A wedding anniversary is the celebration of love, trust, partnership, tolerance and tenacity. The order varies for any given year." —Paul Sweeney

"Oh, the comfort, the inexpressible comfort of feeling safe with a person, having neither to weigh thoughts nor measure words, but pouring them all out, just as they are, chaff and grain together, certain that a faithful hand will take and sift them, keep what is worth keeping, and with a breath of kindness blow the rest away."
—Dinah Craik

"Love does not consist of gazing at each other, but in looking together in the same direction."
—Antoine de Saint-Exupery

"A successful marriage requires falling in love many times, always with the same person."
—Mignon McLaughlin

"Love one another and you will be happy.
It's as simple and as difficult as that."
—Michael Leunig

"It's so great to find that one special person you want to annoy for the rest of your life."—Rita Rudner

"Spouse: someone who'll stand by you through all the trouble you wouldn't have had if you'd stayed single."
—Author Unknown

"Love seems the swiftest, but it is the slowest of growths. No man or woman really knows what perfect love is until they have been married a quarter of a century."
—Mark Twain

"Two such as you with such a master speed
Cannot be parted nor be swept away
From one another once you are agreed
That life is only life forevermore
Together wing to wing and oar to oar."
—Robert Frost

"Love is not blind—it sees more or less,
but because it sees more it is willing to see less."
—Will Moss

"There is no more lovely, friendly, and charming relationship, communion, or company than a good marriage."
—Martin Luther

"Marriage is three parts love and seven parts forgiveness of sins." —Lao Tzu

"My wife and I tried to breakfast together, but we had to stop or our marriage would have been wrecked."
—Winston Churchill

"A great marriage is not when the 'perfect couple' comes together. It is when an imperfect couple learns to enjoy their differences."
—Dave Meurer

"A good marriage is one that allows for change and growth in individuals."
—Pearl Buck

"When a newly married couple smiles, everyone knows why. When a ten-year married couple smiles, everyone wonders why."
—Author Unknown

"Marrying for love may be a bit risky, but it is so honest that God can't help but smile on it."
—Josh Billings

"Love is the thing that enables a woman to sing while she mops up the floor after her husband has walked across it in his barn boots." —Hoosier Farmer

"The bonds of matrimony are like any other bonds—they mature slowly."
—Peter De Vries

"Love is a symbol of eternity. It wipes out all sense of time, destroying all memory of a beginning and all fear of an end."
—Author Unknown

"Are we not like two volumes of one book?"
—Marceline Desbordes-Valmore

"The problem with marriage is that it ends every night after making love, and it must be rebuilt every morning before breakfast."
—Gabriel García Márquez

"A man reserves his true and deepest love not for the species of woman in whose company he finds himself electrified and enkindled, but for that one in whose company he may feel tenderly drowsy."
—George Jean Nathan

"True love stories never have endings."
—Richard Bach

"Nobody has ever measured, even poets,
how much a heart can hold."
—Zelda Fitzgerald

"Often the difference between a successful marriage
and a mediocre one consists of leaving
about three or four things
a day unsaid."
—Harlan Miller

"Love is not the dying moan of a distant violin—
it's the triumphant twang of a bedspring."
—S.J. Perelman

"After about 20 years of marriage, I'm finally starting to scratch the surface of that one. And I think the answer lies somewhere between conversation and chocolate."
—Mel Gibson, about what women want

"Be to her virtues very kind, Be to her faults a little blind."
—Matthew Prior

"Pleasure is the flower that passes;
remembrance, the lasting perfume."
—Jean de Boufflers

"I love being married. It's so great to find that one special person you want to annoy for the rest of your life."
—Rita Rudner

"Marriage is an alliance entered into by a man who can't sleep with the window shut, and a woman who can't sleep with the window open."
—George Bernard Shaw

"Newlyweds become oldyweds, and oldyweds are the reasons that families work."
—Author Unknown

"After the chills and fever of love, how nice is the 98.6° of marriage!"
—Mignon McLaughlin, *The Neurotic's Notebook*, 1960

"My wife says I never listen to her.
At least I think that's what she said."
—Author Unknown

"The man who never in his life
Has washed the dishes with his wife
Or polished up the silver plate—
He still is largely celibate."
—Christopher Morley, washing the dishes

"What counts in making a happy marriage is not so much how compatible you are, but how you deal with incompatibility."
—George Levinger

"The husband who doesn't tell his wife everything probably reasons that what she doesn't know won't hurt him."
—Leo J. Burke

"Married life teaches one invaluable lesson: to think of things far enough ahead not to say them."
—Jefferson Machamer

"A happy marriage is the union of two good forgivers."
—Ruth Bell Graham

"For two people in a marriage to live together day after day is unquestionably the one miracle the Vatican has overlooked."
—Bill Cosby, Love and Marriage

"A happy marriage is a long conversation which always seems too short."
—Andre Maurois

"Marriage is a mistake every man should make."
—George Jessel

"After a few years of marriage, a man can look right at a woman without seeing her—and a woman can see right through a man without looking at him."
—Helen Rowland

"Marriage is three parts love and seven parts forgiveness of sins."
—Langdon Mitchell

Anniversary toasts

A speech should end in a toast. Here are some suggestions:

"Here's to you both
Such a wonderful pair,
On the birthday
of your love affair."

XX years ago you both said "I do"
Down the years, all you've been through
Here's to love, here's to you!

"Heaven give you many, many merry days!"
—Shakespeare, from *The Merry Wives of Windsor*

"To enduring love
And a long, happy life!"

Tenth Anniversary

"Ten years ago you vowed, 'I do'
Both promised to be true,
Today we celebrate with you
And wish you many more years, too!"

Twentieth Anniversary

"A toast to this pair of twenty years
Who've made a life together
Who've stuck together through joys and tears
May your mutual love last forever!"

Twenty-fifth Anniversary

"To abiding love, long may it endure!
Through good times and bad
For richer or poorer,
Sharing and caring, giving and forgiving,
Together always—now that's living!"

Fiftieth Anniversary

"Half a century ago
You both promised to be true.
Your family and friends are here today
To celebrate with you! Congratulations!"

Announcements

If you belong to any kind of group or association, sooner or later you may be called upon to make an announcement, a public statement about something that is going to happen.

Here are some simple guides for making an announcement:

Get their attention

Deliver a sentence or two to create interest and suspense. Wake them up, grab their attention.

Give the lowdown

Provide the name of the program and its purpose. Where, when, who can join, fees etc.

Make the appeal

To join, donate, applaud ...

Give contact details

Phone number, address or email.

Repeat the information

Loudly and clearly and in one sentence give date, time, venue, contact person and contact phone number.

Last thankyou

Example announcement

"Welcome to *Stand and Deliver!*—where you will witness feats of upstanding delivery and outstanding enjoyment.

"*Stand and Deliver!* is a local program committed to the art of public speaking. It is a program that teaches by doing, in a convivial setting. Your club holds its dinner meetings at the Stag Arms Hotel every other Wednesday from 6.30pm to 9pm. Should you wish to join tonight, please approach Jim Spruker at the end of this session.

"I would urge you to consider joining this most effective program. It is said people fear death less than public speaking, but the surprising discovery for all of us who have joined *Stand and Deliver!* is that speaking on public occasions can become the most rewarding and enriching of experiences, not to mention highly enjoyable.

So do approach Jim Spruker who is the man with his hand up at the back of the room—or take one of our brochures on the table by the door. Dinner meetings held Wednesday fortnights, at 6.30pm at the Stag Arms Hotel. Dinner costs $10.00. Joining fees are contained in the brochure.

"Thank you, enjoy your evening."

Eulogies

When somebody passes away, for those who knew and loved that person, it is a difficult and stressful time. People struggle to make meaning of death, and the experience of loss and grief. As a member of the family or a close friend you may be called upon to deliver a eulogy for the deceased at the funeral or memorial service. A eulogy is a short speech that honours the deceased and brings them "to life" for those gathered.

Steps in preparing a eulogy

Gather information:

Curriculum vitae, such as age, marriage dates, children, places lived and so on. Then recollect turns of phrase, mannerisms or typical behaviour which encapsulates the loved one, and talk with others so your eulogy will include their memories as well.

Arrive at a theme:

This helps to tie the threads together when you are talking of that person's life. What were that person's passions? What did they do particularly well? Was it generosity of spirit? Perseverance? Being a nurturer?

Organise your material

Write your notes in point form on file cards, one idea per card. Group the cards into piles on similar topics, then arrange them in logical order.

Draft your speech

Write your first draft. Having access to word processing is useful as it makes the editing process easier. Bridge the various topics with linking sentences. The beginning and ending are most important so give them extra attention. As you write keep the themes of appreciation and celebration in your mind. If appropriate, include touches of humorous affection, elements of lightheartedness.

Rehearse your delivery

The optimum speech time is three to five minutes. Rehearsing helps you to know how long your delivery will take. Remember to breathe and don't be afraid to use pauses. If you are afraid you might break down while reading the eulogy, have someone ready to take over at your signal. Just knowing you have this contingency can help to keep you calm.

Time to speak

When it is your turn to speak, make your way calmly to your speaking position and make your speech. Afterwards, return to your seat. When you are walking, keep your head slightly bowed and avoid too much eye contact with the other attendees.

Excerpts from famous eulogies

Excerpt from Mahatma Gandhi eulogy delivered by Jawarharlal Nehru

"Friends and comrades, the light has gone out of our lives and there is darkness everywhere. I do not know what to tell you and how to say it. Our beloved leader, Bapu as we called him, the father of the nation, is no more…

"The light has gone out, I said, and yet I was wrong. For the light that shone in this country was no ordinary light. The light that has illumined this country for these many years will illumine this country for many more years, and a thousand years later that light will still be seen in this country, and the world will see it and it will give solace to innumerable hearts. For that light represented the living truth… the eternal truths, reminding us of the right path, drawing us from error, taking this ancient country to freedom."

Excerpt from Princess Diana eulogy delivered by her brother Earl Charles Spencer

"Diana was the very essence of compassion, of duty, of style, of beauty. All over the world she was a symbol of selfless humanity. All over the world, a standard bearer for the rights of the truly downtrodden, a very British girl who transcended nationality.

"Someone with a natural nobility who was classless and who proved in the last year that she needed no royal title to continue to generate her particular brand of magic...

"But your greatest gift was your intuition and it was a gift you used wisely. This is what underpinned all your other wonderful attributes and if we look to analyse what it was about you that had such a wide appeal we find it in your instinctive feel for what was really important in all our lives.

"Without your God—given sensitivity we would be immersed in greater ignorance at the anguish of Aids and HIV sufferers, the plight of the homeless, the isolation of lepers, the random destruction of landmines.

"Diana explained to me once that it was her innermost feelings of suffering that made it possible for her to connect with her constituency of the rejected.

"And here we come to another truth about her. For all the status, the glamour, the applause, Diana remained throughout a very insecure person at heart, almost childlike in her desire to do good for others so she could release herself from deep feelings of unworthiness of which her eating disorders were merely a symptom.

"The world sensed this part of her character and cherished her for her vulnerability whilst admiring her for her honesty."

Excerpt from John F. Kennedy Funeral Eulogy by Senator Jacob Javits by Senator Jacob Javits at a Senate Memorial Service (December 1963)

"Words cannot describe how the American people felt when they lost their president. Not until the vacuum of disbelief was filled with the horror of comprehension did any of us realize how much we identified ourselves, even apart from personal friendship, with the president—this intellectual, vigorous young man— and he would have been that if he were eighty—expressing the very essence of the youthfulness of our nation...

"As a nation, we have lost a president who understood the institution of the presidency, gloried in its overwhelming responsibilities, and discharged his duties with dash and joy, which were an inspiration to the youth of our nation.

"But John F. Kennedy was more than that. He was a man filled with the joy of living. He was a husband, a father—and my friend...

"He was vigorous and healthy and smiling and friendly—a complete human being, concerned about other human beings who were no longer as vigorous and not quite as healthy as they used to be."

Excerpt from JFK jr. eulogy by Teddy Kennedy, his uncle

"Once, when they asked John what he would do if he went into politics and was elected president, he said, 'I guess the first thing is call up Uncle Teddy and gloat.' I loved that. It was so like his father.

"From the first day of his life, John seemed to belong not only to our family, but to the American family. The whole world knew his name before he did. A famous photograph showed John racing across the lawn as his father landed in the White House helicopter and swept up John in his arms. When my brother saw that photo, he exclaimed, 'Every mother in the United States is saying, 'Isn't it wonderful to see that love between a son and his father, the way that John races to be with his father.' Little do they know, that son would have raced right by his father to get to that helicopter.

"John had amazing grace. He accepted who he was, but he cared more about what he could and should become. He saw things that could be lost in the glare of the spotlight. And he could laugh at the absurdity of too much pomp and circumstance.

"John was also the son who was once protected by his mother. He went on to become her pride—and then her protector in her final days. He was the Kennedy who loved us all, but who especially cherished his sister Caroline, celebrated her brilliance, and took strength and joy from their lifelong mutual admiration society. And for a thousand days, he was a husband who adored the wife who became his perfect soul mate. John's father taught us all to reach for the moon and the stars. John did that in all he did—and he found his shining star when he married Carolyn ...
"John was a serious man who brightened our lives with his smile and his grace. He was a son of privilege who founded a program called Reaching Up to train better caregivers for the mentally disabled. He joined Wall Street executives on the Robin Hood Foundation to help the city's impoverished children. And he did it all so quietly, without ever calling attention to himself.

John was one of Jackie's two miracles. He was still becoming the person he would be, and doing it by the beat of his own drummer. He had only just begun. There was in him a great promise of things to come."

Excerpt from Rev Dr. Martin Luther King Funeral Eulogy by Robert Kennedy

"I have bad news for you, for all our fellow citizens, and people who love peace all over the world, and that is that Martin Luther King was shot and killed tonight.

"Martin Luther King dedicated his life to love and to justice for his fellow human beings, and he died because of that effort...

"For those of you who are black and are tempted to be filled with hatred and distrust at the injustice of such an act, against all white people, I can only say that I feel in my own heart the same kind of feeling. I had a member of my family killed, but a white man killed him. But we have to make an effort in the United States, we have to make an effort to understand, to go beyond these rather difficult times.

"My favourite poet was Aeschylus. He wrote: 'In our sleep pain which cannot forget falls drop by drop upon the heart until, in our own despair, against our will, comes wisdom through the awful grace of God.'

"We've had difficult times in the past. We will have difficult times in the future. It is not the end of violence; it is not the end of lawlessness; it is not the end of disorder.

"But the vast majority of white people and the vast majority of black people in this country want to live together, want to improve the quality of our life, and want justice for all human beings who abide in our land. Let us dedicate ourselves to what the Greeks wrote so many years ago: to tame the savageness of man and to make gentle the life of this world.

"Let us dedicate ourselves to that, and say a prayer for our country and for our people."

Excerpt from Robert Kennedy eulogy delivered by brother Teddy Kennedy

"...Love is not an easy feeling to put into words. Nor is loyalty, or trust or joy. But he was all of these. He loved life completely and lived it intensely.

"A few years back, Robert Kennedy wrote some words about his own father and they expressed the way we in his family feel about him. He said of what his father meant to him: 'What it really all adds up to is love—not love as it is described with such facility in popular magazines, but the kind of love that is affection and respect, order, encouragement, and support. Our awareness of this was an incalculable source of strength, and because real love is something unselfish and involves sacrifice and giving, we could not help but profit from it.

"Beneath it all, he has tried to engender a social conscience. There were wrongs, which needed attention. There were people who were poor and who needed help. And we have a responsibility to them and to this country. Through no virtues and accomplishments of our own, we have been fortunate enough to be born in the United States under the most comfortable conditions. We, therefore, have a responsibility to others who are less well off"

"…My brother need not be idealized, or enlarged in death beyond what he was in life, to be remembered simply as a good and decent man, who saw wrong and tried to right it, saw suffering and tried to heal it, saw war and tried to stop it.

Those of us who loved him and who take him to his rest today, pray that what he was to us and what he wished for others will some day come to pass for all the world.

As he said many times, in many parts of this nation, to those he touched and who sought to touch him:

'*Some men see things as they are and say why.*
I dream things that never were and say why not.' "

Excerpt from Marilyn Monroe eulogy by Lee Strasberg

"Marilyn Monroe was a legend.

"In her own lifetime she created a myth of what a poor girl from a deprived background could attain. For the entire world she became a symbol of the eternal feminine.

"But I have no words to describe the myth and the legend. I did not know this Marilyn Monroe.

"We gathered here today, knew only Marilyn—a warm human being, impulsive and shy, sensitive and in fear of rejection, yet ever avid for life and reaching out for fulfilment."

"...The dream of her talent, which she had nurtured as a child, was not a mirage. When she first came to me I was amazed at the startling sensitivity which she possessed and which had remained fresh and undimmed, struggling to express itself despite the life to which she had been subjected. Others were as physically beautiful as she was, but there was obviously something more in her, something that people saw and recognized in her performances and with which they identified. She had a luminous quality—a combination of wistfulness, radiance, yearning—to set her apart and yet make everyone wish to be a part of it, to share in the childish way which was so shy and yet so vibrant.

"Now it is at an end. I hope her death will stir sympathy and understanding for a sensitive artist and a woman who brought joy and pleasure to the world.

"I cannot say goodbye. Marilyn never liked goodbyes, but in the peculiar way she had of turning things around so that they faced reality—I will say au revoir. For the country to which she has gone, we must all someday visit."

Excerpts from anonymous eulogies

A Brother

"My brother saw good in everyone. He taught us all the meaning of tolerance and forgiveness. It is up to us to practice the lessons he was with us to teach."

"My baby brother, six foot five (inches) and bigger than life, you were always the one I could look up to. May you rest in peace. No time or space can erase your image and importance to us."

A father

"Dad you were my idol. You taught me well. It is my turn to pass on your lessons to my children and grandchildren."

"You were a loving, responsible man."

"Dad, your suffering is over. Sleep on in the arms of Jesus. We shall meet again in Heaven."

Suicide Deaths

"May she find the peace in Heaven that she could not find even with our determined and loving efforts, in life on Earth."

"Ours is not to explain or perhaps even to understand, but to go on loving his memory and living the life on his behalf that he so wanted for himself but could not achieve."

Quotes for eulogies

Beginning your eulogy with a quote or short poem, or ending with one can be very powerful. Choose something which speaks to you and has meaning for the life of the deceased and those who have known and loved that person. Here are a collection of possible quotes you may choose to use.

"Do not stand at my grave and weep
I am not there, I do not sleep
I am a thousand winds that blow,
I am the diamond glint on snow.
I am the sunlight on ripened grain,
I am the gentle autumn rain,
When you wake in the morning hush
I am the swift, uplifting rush
Of quiet birds in circling flight.
I am the soft starlight at night.
Do not stand at my grave and cry
I am not there—I did not die."
—Mary Frye

"To live in hearts we leave behind
Is not to die."
—Thomas Campbell, *Hallowed Ground*

"As a well-spent day brings happy sleep, so a life well used brings happy death." —Leonardo da Vinci

"If I should go before the rest of you,
Break not a flower nor inscribe a stone.
Nor when I'm gone speak in a Sunday voice,
But be the usual selves that I have known.
Weep, if you must,
Parting is hell.
But life goes one,
So sing as well."
—Author unknown

"Because I could not stop for Death,
He kindly stopped for me.
The Carriage held but just ourselves
And Immortality."
—Emily Dickinson

"For what is it to die,
But to stand in the sun and melt into the wind?"
—Kahlil Gibran, from *The Prophet*

"We understand death for the first time when he puts his hand upon one whom we love."
—Madame de Stael

"The death of someone we know always reminds us that we are still alive—perhaps for some purpose which we ought to re-examine."
—Mignon McLaughlin, *The Neurotic's Notebook*, 1960

"Life is eternal, and love is immortal,
and death is only a horizon;
and a horizon is nothing save the limit of our sight."
—Rossiter Worthington Raymond

"Death leaves a heartache no one can heal, love leaves a memory no one can steal."
—from a headstone in Ireland

"We must embrace pain and burn it as fuel for our journey."
—Kenji Miyazawa

"When you are sorrowful look again in your heart,
and you shall see that in truth you are weeping
for that which has been your delight." —Kahlil Gibran

"It's so curious: one can resist tears and 'behave' very well in the hardest hours of grief. But then someone makes you a friendly sign behind a window, or one notices that a flower that was in bud only yesterday has suddenly blossomed, or a letter slips from a drawer…and everything collapses." —Colette

"Give sorrow words; the grief that does not speak whispers the o'er—fraught heart and bids it break."
—William Shakespeare

"Man, when he does not grieve, hardly exists."
—Antonio Porchia, *Voces*, 1943

"Sorrow makes us all children again—destroys all differences of intellect. The wisest know nothing." —Ralph Waldo Emerson

"Grief is itself a medicine." —William Cowper, *Charity*

"Memory is a way of holding onto the things you love, the things you are, the things you never want to lose."
—From the television show *The Wonder Years*

"We acquire the strength we have to overcome."
—Ralph Waldo Emerson

"You can clutch the past so tightly to your chest that it leaves your arms too full to embrace the present." —Jan Glidewell

"There are things that we don't want to happen but have to accept, things we don't want to know but have to learn, and people we can't live without but have to let go."
—Author Unknown

"In the night of death, hope sees a star, and listening love can hear the rustle of a wing." —Robert Ingersoll

"Even if happiness forgets you a little bit,
never completely forget about it."
—Jacques Prévert

"He who has gone, so we but cherish his memory, abides with us, more potent, nay, more present than the living man."
—Antoine de Saint-Exupery

"Oh heart, if one should say to you that the soul perishes like the body, answer that the flower withers, but the seed remains."
—Kahlil Gibran

"Love here on earth
Love beyond the grave
There are no roads
My love for you can't pave."
—T. Sachs

"Good-night! good-night! as we so oft have said
Beneath this roof at midnight, in the days
That are no more, and shall no more return.
Thou hast but taken up thy lamp and gone to bed;
I stay a little longer, as one stays
To cover up the embers that still burn."
—Henry Wadsworth Longfellow

"For death is no more than a turning of us over from time to eternity." —William Penn

"Years, following years, steal something every day;
At last they steal us from ourselves away."
—Horace

"Gaily I lived as ease and nature taught,
And spent my little life without a thought,
And am amazed that Death, that tyrant grim,
Should think of me, who never thought of him."
—René Francois Regnier

"The fear of death follows from the fear of life.
A man who lives fully is prepared to die at any time."
—Mark Twain

"The day which we fear as our last
is but the birthday of eternity." —Seneca

"They tell us that suicide is the greatest piece of cowardice…that suicide is wrong; when it is quite obvious that there is nothing in the world to which every man has a more unassailable title than to his own life and person."
—Arthur Schopenhauer

"He who has gone, so we but cherish his memory, abides with us, more potent, nay, more present than the living man."
—Antoine de Saint-Exupery

"People living deeply have no fear of death."
—Anaïs Nin, *Diary*, 1967

"To die proudly when it is no longer possible to live proudly. Death of one's own free choice, death at the proper time, with a clear head and with joyfulness, consummated in the midst of children and witnesses: so that an actual leave—taking is possible while he who is leaving is still there."
—Friedrich Nietzsche, *Expeditions of an Untimely Man*

"Suicide is man's way of telling God,
'You can't fire me—I quit'. "
—Bill Maher, on *Politically Incorrect*, 1995

Suicide is…the sincerest form of criticism life gets.
—Wilfred Sheed, *The Good Word*, 1978

Graduation speeches

As a graduate you are part of a group that has shared significant achievements and history. There is much material if you reflect on these life-changing formative years of study and the friendships forged with your peers and your teachers.

Three parts to the speech

Introduction

Begin by grabbing their attention—a quote, an anecdote or a word image. Tell them what it means to you to be able to speak on this occasion. Provide your theme and outline the few points you wish to cover.

Body of speech

1. Past

Recollections of events or occasions: fun /tears—trials/ tribulations—create vivid word pictures of significant events for the school or college, the character building, the sense of solidarity and commitment.

2. Present

Begin with "We are here tonight to celebrate the accomplishments..." or words to that effect. And state clearly all you wish to say about this momentous occasion.

3. Future

Paint a word picture, which will give context to the graduates taking their learning out into the wider world and the impact their qualifications may have upon the future.

Conclusion

Summarise your three key points—past, present and future. Revisit your introduction and restate the overall theme, which could have been about the institution of learning, the quality of education or the application this student group showed in keeping their commitment and vision.

Graduation quotes

"You cannot help but learn more as you take the world into your hands. Take it up reverently, for it is an old piece of clay, with millions of thumbprints on it."
—John Updike

"School's out, Memories past, Don't ever doubt, Our friendship will last."—Unknown

"Education is what survives
when what has been learned has been forgotten."
—B.F. Skinner

"It is the mark of an educated mind to be able to entertain a thought without accepting it."
—Aristotle

"Genius is the gold in the mine; talent is the miner that works to bring it out." —Lady Blessington

"Graduation is only a concept. In real life every day you graduate. Graduation is a process that goes on until the last day of your life. If you can grasp that, you'll make a difference."
—Arie Pencovici

"It's not your blue blood, your pedigree or your college degree. It's what you do with your life that counts."
—Millard Fuller

"The trouble with learning from experience is that you never graduate."
—Doug Larson

"Your families are extremely proud of you. You can't imagine the sense of relief they are experiencing. This would be a most opportune time to ask for money."
—Gary Bolding

"The advantage of a classical education is that it enables you to despise the wealth that it prevents you from achieving."
—Russell Green

"Your schooling may be over, but remember that your education still continues."
—Anonymous

"If I made you laugh, you're welcome.
If I made you cry, I'm sorry.
If I changed your life,
chances are you've done the same for me."
—From an educator

"I have learned this at least by my experiment;
that if one advances confidently in the direction of his dream,
and endeavours to live the life which he had imagines,
he will meet with a success unexpected in common hours."
—Henry David Thoreau

"The important thing is not to stop questioning."
—Albert Einstein

"Be who you are and say what you feel,
because those who mind don't matter
and those who matter don't mind."
—Dr. Seuss

"If opportunity doesn't knock, build a door."
—Milton Berle

"Don't live down to expectations.
Go out there and do something remarkable."
—Wendy Wasserstein

"Be careful to leave your sons well instructed rather than rich,
for the hopes of the instructed
are better than the wealth of the ignorant."
—Epictetus

"The things taught in schools and colleges are not an education,
but the means of education."
—Ralph Waldo Emerson

"We know what we are, but know not what we may be."
—William Shakespeare

"To accomplish great things, we must dream as well as act."
—Anatole France

"The supreme end of education is expert discernment in all things -- the power to tell the good from the bad, the genuine from the counterfeit, and to prefer the good and the genuine to the bad and the counterfeit."
—Samuel Johnson

"Education makes a people easy to lead, but difficult to drive,
easy to govern, but impossible to enslave."
—Lord Brougham

"The man who graduates today and stops learning tomorrow is uneducated the day after."
—Newton D. Baker

"Knowledge will forever govern ignorance: and a people who mean to be their own governors, must arm themselves with the power which knowledge gives."
—James Madison

"The direction in which education starts a man will determine his future." —Plato

"The most important aspect of freedom of speech is freedom to learn. All education is a continuous dialogue— questions and answers that pursue every problem on the horizon. That is the essence of academic freedom."
—William O. Douglas

"Education is the process by which the individual relates himself to the universe, gives himself citizenship in the changing world, shares the race's mind and enfranchises his own soul."
—John H. Finley

"When you know a thing, to hold that you know it, and when you do not know a thing, to allow that you do not know it: this is knowledge." —Confucius

"Education is the best provision for old age."
—Aristotle

"Whoso neglects learning in his youth
Loses the past and is dead for the future."
—Euripides

"A college education is not a quantitative body of memorised knowledge salted away in a card file. It is a taste for knowledge, a taste for philosophy, if you will; a capacity to explore, to question to perceive relationships, between fields of knowledge and experience."
—A. Whitney Griswold

"You are educated.
Your certification is in your degree.
You may think of it as the ticket to the good life.
Let me ask you to think of an alternative.
Think of it as your ticket to change the world."
—Tom Brokaw

"The fireworks begin today.
Each diploma is a lighted match,
each one of you is a fuse."
—Ed Koch

"Graduation is not the end; it's the beginning."
—Orrin Hatch

"It is clear the future holds great opportunities. It also holds pitfalls. The trick will be to avoid the pitfalls, seize the opportunities, and get back home by six o'clock."
— Woody Allen

"The whole purpose of education is to turn mirrors into windows."
—Sydney Harris

"The best helping hand that you will ever receive is the one at the end of your own arm."
—Fred Dehner

Introductions

The purpose of an introductory speech is to form a bridge between the audience and the guest speaker. Whether the guest speaker is someone they know well or a complete stranger, the introduction is still a necessary elememt for setting the scene and preparing the audience.

Here are some simple pointers:

1. Begin by allowing the audience to know of the presence of the honoured guest at this meeting (without letting slip the name)
2. Build up that person's profile by giving their personal and professional information in a systematic manner.
3. End by highlighting and announcing THE NAME OF THE VIP.

Example of an ending:

"It is my great pleasure to present to you, The Chairman of the WE CARE FOR YOU foundation and author of 'Can't Do Enough' , Mr Con Passion."

The don'ts of an introduction

DON'T disclose the name until the very end.

DON''T speak for more than three minutes.

DON'T give false praise—it demeans the speaker.

DON'T use hackneyed language such as "he's great this, great that, one and only, none other than, and so on".

Importance of humour

To disarm your audience, begin with an injection of humour—it's sure to get their attention.

Our next speaker needs no introduction

"Coming up next week is a man who needs no introduction. However, he insists upon it."

"He needs no introduction. What he needs is a conclusion."

"Rule number two in public speaking: After a very flattering introduction, never tell the audience you don't deserve it. They'll find out soon enough."

"Our next speaker says he was born during the great depression. Not the country's—his mother's."

"Our next speaker says she will give you in length what she lacks in depth."

"You've heard of many speakers who need no introduction. Here's one who doesn't deserve one."

"He hasn't got much to say but at least he doesn't try and say anything else."—Robert Benchley

"I could say many nice things about our next speaker, but I'd rather be honest."

"There are some speakers who need no introduction. But our next speaker needs as much help as he can get."

"I've heard it said about our next speaker that no matter what you pay him, he's worth every penny. He's speaking tonight for free. So don't get your hopes up."

"What can I say about our next speaker that he probably hasn't already said about himself?"

"And now, a man who has made anonymity a household name…"

"And now, a man who wears his heart on his sleeve, and spaghetti sauce on his tie…"

"And now, I introduce a man who has seen it all, but has understood very little of it."

"And now, I introduce a man who is clever and witty, and I could go on and on, except I'm having a terrible time reading his handwriting."

"Although our speaker eventually became a model, she says she wasn't the cutest child. In fact, her parents threw away her kindergarten photo and framed the negative."

"Before we begin the program, I want to point out the exits in case the fire alarm goes off—or a speaker won't get off."

"Before we introduce our next speaker, let me remind you that no one is perfect."

"Character, integrity, principle. People want to know why he hasn't run for public office. I just told you."

"He was nervous when I told him to speak tonight. He said, 'What if they boo me?' I said, 'Don't be silly! People can't boo and yawn at the same time.'"

"He's been voted one of the finest minds in (add location), which is a lot like being named to the ten best-dressed list in Russia."

"He's done so many wonderful things in such a brief time, it's hard to exaggerate his accomplishments—but I'll do my best."

"Here is a man who has done more for banquet audiences than the Titanic did for the winter cruise business."

"Here is a man who is ahead of his time, but let's not make a big deal over three or four minutes."

"Here's a man who is world famous in certain parts of the country."

"I could stand up here for an hour and talk about our next speaker's accomplishments—but only if I talked really, really slowly."

"I have been told that the mind cannot absorb any more than the seat can tolerate."

"I'd like to introduce one of the foremost jugglers of our time—our treasurer!"

"I'll begin by telling you what a remarkable person our speaker is. Then I'll describe all the wonderful things he's done for the community. And I'll conclude by saying some things that are true."

"I'm glad to be here. I followed the Toastmaster's instructions but I got here anyway."

"I'm not making a speech tonight, so I won't put you to sleep. But after the other speakers are finished, I will wake you up."

"In introducing our treasurer, the good news is he's as honest as the day is long. The bad news is that for the last five years, he's been working the night shifts."

"In your office we have someone who's always there...a person we can count on...someone who does the work of three people—your secretary."

"Many of you came here tonight looking for a dynamic speech, a good meal, a pleasant evening. And I hope you get one of them."

"Our next speaker has been compared to Benjamin Franklin. Some people think he ought to go fly a kite."

"Our speaker can point to many amazing accomplishments in his lifetime. Unfortunately, none of them were his."

"Our next speaker says she will give you in length what she lacks in depth."

"Thank you for those fine opening comments. I'm sure your thoughts, like tonight's dinner, will stay with us for a long time."

"Throughout his many years, he has always taken the road less travelled. Some say it's because he's independent, creative and adventurous. His wife says it's because he never asks for directions."

"We have many speakers tonight, so I won't spend time telling funny stories you won't believe. I'll get right to the introductions you won't believe."

Speaker responds after a bad introduction

"Thank you. I'm happy to be here—after that introduction, I'm happy to be anywhere."

"Thank you. I must tell you, I've received much worse introductions than that…and from much better people"

"Thank you. I'm happy to be here having survived that introduction."

"I thought that was a very creative and funny introduction. I can't wait to tell my attorney and see if he agrees.

"Do you realize, if I were one of those speakers who need no introduction, we would have been home by now" (after a very long introduction).

Speaker responds after a good introduction

"That was a wonderful introduction. Now even I can't wait to hear what I have to say."

"I wish you hadn't called me a self-made man. Up till now I've been trying to share the blame."

"After an introduction like that, anything I do now is a comeback."

"Whenever I get a big build up like that I make it a practice never to tell an audience I don't deserve it. I figure they're going to find that out soon enough."

"That's the most flattering introduction I've ever received. And you read it just the way I wrote it."

"That was a very gracious introduction. In fact, I'm sorry I have to speak now. I'd rather sit here all night and listen to your introductions."

Retirement Speeches

From the retiree

This speech should be light-hearted, sincere and gracious in tone. The touch of nostalgia doesn't go astray—"When I first joined the company…" highlighting how different work life has become over the years. You could include remembrance of past colleagues and the growth of the company over your years of service.

Matters you could include:

* Make your opening interesting by starting with a pithy or humorous quote . For example, "Throughout my working life I followed a few simple rules: When in charge, meditate. When in doubt, mumble. When in difficulty, delegate."
* Mention an incident from your working life—it could be humorous or momentous—your very first day, your first promotion or the introduction of computerisation.
* Show appreciation to the well-wishers and any gifts you might have received.
* Mention your plans for the future—whether you plan to go travelling, improve your golf handicap or take on a consultancy.
* Thank the family member or staff member for organising the party.
* Mention the mentor or colleagues who made a difference to your working life.
* Finish with a touch of lightheartedness or a quote about not forgetting old friends and making the most of retirement.

By a colleague

Make the speech sincere and personal, whilst still keeping the tone lighthearted and upbeat. Do your homework—find out something about the retiree—the highlights of their working life, talents and skills, plans for the future.

Matters you could include:

* Capture the audience's attention with an opening. For instance, Vince Lombardi once said, "the harder you work, the harder it is to surrender and this is surely true of John Doe."
* Refer to the retiree's contribution to the company, organisation— if possible, be specific—focus on the good points, the strengths.
* Mention an incident during the retiree's working life—getting tips from someone who shared the years with them is useful.
* Including a funny anecdote or story always helps.
* Make a presentation of the retirement gift.
* End with best wishes for the future and a toast to the retiree.

Retirement quotes

"When you retire, think and act as if you were still working; when you're still working, think and act a bit as if you were already retired." —Anonymous

"I am a free man. I feel as light as a feather."
—Javier Perez De Cuellar

"There are some who start their retirement long before they stop working." —Robert Half

"When a man retires, his wife gets twice the husband but only half the income."
—Chi Chi Rodriguez, Puerto Rican golfer

"It is time I stepped aside for a less experienced and less able man." —Professor Scott Elledge

"The question isn't at what age I want to retire, it's at what income."
—George Foreman

"Age is only a number, a cipher for the records. A man can't retire his experience. He must use it. Experience achieves more with less energy and time." —Bernard M. Baruch

"Musicians don't retire;
they stop when there's no more music in them."
—Louis Armstrong

"There are an enormous number of managers who have retired on the job." —Peter F. Drucker

"Retirement at sixty-five is ridiculous. When I was sixty-five I still had pimples." —George Burns

"Work is the recreation of the retired." —Anonymous

"Retirement : Statutory senility."
—Emmett O'Donnell

"Don't simply retire from something;
have something to retire to."—Harry Emerson Fosdick

"I will not retire while I've still got my legs
and my make-up box." —Bette Davis

"I have never liked working.
To me a job is an invasion of privacy."
—Danny McGoorty

"And in the end it's not the years in your life that count.
It's the life in your years." —Abraham Lincoln

"A man's only as old as the woman he feels."
—Groucho Marx

"I don't feel old. I don't feel anything until noon.
Then it's time for my nap."
—Bob Hope

"I don't plan to grow old gracefully. I plan to have face-lifts until my ears meet." —Rita Rudner

"I do wish I could tell you my age but it's impossible.
It keeps changing all the time."
—Greer Garson

"I'm very pleased to be here. Let's face it, at my age I'm very pleased to be anywhere."
—George Burns

"The secret of longevity is…to keep breathing."
—Sophie Tucker

"At my age I do what Mark Twain did. I get my daily paper, look at the obituaries page and if I'm not there I carry on as usual."
—Patrick Moore

"Retire from work, but not from life."
—M.K. Soni

"I don't want to achieve immortality through my work,
I want to achieve it through not dying."
—Woody Allen

"As we grow older, our bodies get shorter
and our anecdotes longer." —Robert Quillen

"Retirement, a time to do what you want to do,
when you want to do it." —Catherine Pulsifer

"We make a living by what we get,
we make a life by what we give."
—Sir Winston Churchill

"Life is no brief candle to me.
It is a sort of splendid torch which I have got a hold of for the moment, and I want to make it burn as brightly as possible before handing it on to future generations."
—George Bernard Shaw

Retirement Toasts

"Happy the man, and happy he alone,
He who can call today his own, He who, secure within can say,
Tomorrow do thy worst, for I have lived today."

"Merry met, and merry part,
I drink to thee with all my heart."

"To your retirement.
A well-deserved reward for a job well done."

"To a man who always has his foot to the pedal, his shoulder to the wheel, and his nose to the grindstone. How he got any work done in that position I'll never know."

"May you taste the sweetest pleasures that fortune ere bestowed, and may all your friends remember all the favours you are owed."

"You're not too old when your hair turns grey,
You're not too old when your teeth decay.
But you'll know you're awaiting that final sleep,
When your mind makes promises your body can't keep."

"May you always have a cool head and a warm heart.
May life give you more than you can ever eat."

"Let's raise our glasses to the one that got away!"

"The first few months of retirement are the hardest. That's when the husband asks, 'What in the world did you do all day when I was at work?' And the wife replies, 'Better.'"

'It's with joy and sadness
that we say farewell tonight
No one more loved or respected
has earned this right."

"Here's to the holidays — all 365 of them!"

"I won't go into how many mistakes he made during his xxxx years of service with our company, but as a token of our esteem and admiration, we've had his eraser bronzed."

"What can I tell you about him, He's just a terrific guy
I cannot remember his good points,
but his wife asked me to try."

"He's so old that when he asks for a three-minute egg, they ask for the money up front."

Retirement Jokes

"Retirement is when your wife realizes she never gave your secretary enough sympathy."

"Retirement is when Memory Lane becomes a Freeway."

"He would always listen to our troubles.
Why not, he caused most of them."

"He's lived a long life and doesn't use glasses—he drinks straight from the bottle."

"Retirement is when you go from spending six hours in your garden for the exercise to spending thirty hours in your garden for the food."

"Retirement is when you have this total sense of freedom. You almost feel like picking up the phone and dialing the office to call in 'well'."

"Retirees were even mentioned in the Bible. Remember that story about the multitude that loafs and fishes?"

Golfer's Joke

An 80-year-old man goes to the doctor for a checkup. The doctor is amazed at what good shape the guy is in and asks, "How do you stay in such great physical condition?"

"I'm a golfer," says the old guy, "and that's why I'm in such good shape. I'm up well before daylight and out golfing up and down the fairways."

"Well," says the doctor, "I'm sure that helps, but there's got to be more to it. How old was your dad when he died?"

"Who said my dad's dead?"

The doctor is amazed. "You mean you're 80 years old and your dad's still alive. How old is he?"

"He's 100 years old," says the old golfer. "In fact he golfed with me this morning, and that's why he's still alive. He's a golfer too."

"Well," the doctor says, "that's great, but I'm sure there's more to it than that. How about your dad's dad? How old was he when he died?"

"Who said my grandpa's dead?"

Stunned, the doctor asks, "You mean you're 80 years old and your granfather is still living! Incredible, how old is he?"

"He's 118 years old," says the old golfer.

The doctor is getting frustrated at this point, "So, I guess he went golfing with you this morning too?"

"No. Grandpa couldn't go this morning because he's getting married today."

At this point the doctor is close to losing it. "Getting married!! Why would a 118 year-old guy want to get married?"

"Who said he wanted to?"

Doctor's Advice

Percy, an 82 year-old man, went to the doctor to get a physical.

A few days later the doctor saw Percy walking down the street with a gorgeous young lady on his arm.

A couple of days later the doctor spoke to Percy and said,

'You're really doing great, aren't you?'

Percy replied, 'Just doing what you said, Doctor: Get a hot mamma and be cheerful.'

The doctor said, 'I didn't say that. I said, 'You got a heart murmur. Be careful.'"

Special birthdays

The content of birthday speeches can vary quite a lot depending on how many years there are on the "odometer". It is possible, however, to devise a model outline for any birthday speech, whether it be their 21st or 101st.

1. Start by welcoming the birthday guest.
2. Tell a story or two which reveal his/her remarkable qualities and do it from an unexpected but positive angle.
3. Show appreciation for that person's role in the family, and with friends and colleagues.
4. Congratulate the birthday guest. Wish him/her love, health, success and many happy returns. Do this in the form of a toast.

Affectionate humour and mild teasing are a welcome component of the birthday speech. Find a quote or tailor a joke or rely upon anecdotes which show the guests the human side of the birthday person.

General birthday toasts

"Here we stand and raise our glasses
And drink to the health of the birthday boy/girl
We love you and wish you well!"

"Your friends and family are gathered here
Because it's that special day of the year
Happy Birthday to you, and many returns!"

"A toast to you!
May your special day be full of fun,
With well wishes and presents from everyone!
On this the anniversary of your birth
We drink to you and praise your…beauty!"

"Hip hip hooray
A toast to you on your birthday!"

"A toast to the reason for this party
To his/ her wealth and keeping hearty!"

Special birthday toasts and quotes

Twenty

"Then come kiss me, sweet and twenty,
Youth's a stuff will not endure"

—William Shakespeare,
Twelfth Night

Twenty - One

"Today you have turned twenty-one
We've gathered to wish you the best
To reflect on the years that got you here
And talk of the future and the rest!"

A 21st birthday joke

A man is waiting for his wife to give birth. The doctor comes in and informs the dad that his son was born without torso, arms or legs. The son is just a head!

But the dad loves his son and raises him as well as he can, with love and compassion.

After 21 years, the son is now old enough for his first drink. Dad takes him to the bar, tearfully tells the son he is proud of him and orders up the biggest, strongest drink for his boy.

With all the bar patrons looking on curiously and the bartender shaking his head in disbelief, the boy takes his first sip of alcohol.

Swoop! A torso pops out! The bar is dead silent; then bursts into a whoop of joy. The father, shocked, begs his son to drink again. The patrons chant "Take another drink!" The bartender still shakes his head in dismay.

Swoop! Two arms pops out. The bar goes wild. The father, crying and wailing, begs his son to drink again. The patrons chant "Take another drink!" The bartender ignores the whole affair. By now the boy is getting tipsy, and with his new hands he reaches down, grabs his drink and guzzles the last of it.

Swoop! Two legs pop out. The bar is in chaos. The father falls to his knees and tearfully thanks God. The boy stands up on his new legs and stumbles to the left...then to the right...right through the front door, into the street, where a truck runs over him and kills him instantly.

The bar falls silent.

The father moans in grief.

The bartender sighs and says…

(wait for it)

(it's coming)

(take a deep breath)

"He should have quit while he was a head!"

A 21st poem

"When I was one-and-twenty
I heard a wise man say,
'Give crowns and pounds and guineas
But not your heart away;
Give pearls away and rubies
But keep your fancy free.'
But I was one-and-twenty,
No use to talk to me.

When I was one-and-twenty
I heard him say again,
'The heart out of the bosom
Was never given in vain;
'Tis paid with sighs a plenty
And sold for endless rue.'
And I am two-and-twenty,
And oh, 'tis true, 'tis true."

Thirty

"The best ten years of a woman's life are between
twenty-nine and thirty."

"Thirty isn't so bad. Lots of people would love to be thirty…
Especially the ones who are forty!

"For a young man, a woman of thirty has irresistible attractions."
—Honore De Balzac

"Everything I know I learned after I was thirty."
—Georges Clemenceau

"Time and Tide wait for no man,
but time always stands still for a woman of thirty."
—Robert Frost

Thirty five

"Thirty five is a very attractive age;
London society is full of women who have of their own
free choice remained thirty-five for years."
—Oscar Wilde

Forty

"What most persons consider as virtue,
after the age of 40 is simply a loss of energy."
—Voltaire

"Life begins at forty."
—W. B. Pitkin

"This wine is forty years old. It certainly doesn't show its age."
Latin: *Hoc vinum Falernum annorum quadragenta est.*
Bene aetatem fert.
—Cicero

"The first forty years of life give us the text:
the next thirty supply the commentary."
—Arthur Schopenhauer

"Every man over forty is a scoundrel."
—George Bernard Shaw

"Be wise with speed;
A fool at forty is a fool indeed."
—Edward Young

"Forty is the old age of youth; fifty is the youth of old age."
—French Proverb

Fifty

"The years between fifty and seventy are the hardest. You are always being asked to do things, and yet you are not decrepit enough to turn them down."
—T.S. Eliot

"At twenty, you want to be the master of your fate and the captain of your soul. At fifty you settle is you're the master of your weight and the captain of your bowling team!"
—Anonymous

"At age fifty, everyone has the face he deserves."
—George Orwell

"The man who views the world at fifty the same as he did at twenty has wasted thirty years of his life."
—Muhammad Ali

"A man shouldn't fool with booze until he's fifty
And then he's a damn fool if he doesn't."
—William Faulkner

Sixty

"A man of sixty has spent twenty years in bed and over three years in eating." —Arnold Bennett

"Looking fifty is great—if you're sixty." —Joan Rivers

"What, start at this! when sixty years have spread
Their grey experience o'er thy hoary head?
Is this the all observing age could gain?
Or hast thou known the world so long in vain?"
—John Dryden

"One starts to get young at the age of sixty
and then it is too late."
—Pablo Picasso

Getting older quotes

"Birthdays are good for you. The more you have, the longer you live." —Unknown

"Gather ye rosebuds while ye may
Old Time is still aflying
And this same flower that smiles today
Tomorrow will be dying."
—Robert Herrick

"You've reached middle age when all you exercise is caution."
—Anon

"Middle age is youth without its levity and age without decay."
—Anon

"A diplomat is a man who always remembers a woman's birthday but never remembers her age."
—Robert Frost

"Old age: A great sense of calm and freedom. When the passions have relaxed their hold, you may have escaped, not from one master but from many."
—Plato

"No wise man ever wished to be younger."
—Jonathan Swift

"One of the signs of passing youth is the birth of a sense of fellowship with other human beings as we take our place among them. "
—Virginia Woolf

"May you live all the days of your life."
—Jonathan Swift

"The best birthdays of all are those that haven't arrived yet."
—Robert Orben

"Grow old along with me!
The best is yet to be, the last of life,
for which the first was made."
—Robert Browning

"Inside every older person is a younger person—
wondering what the hell happened."
—Cora Harvey Armstrong

"To me, old age is always 15 years older than I am."
—Bernard Baruch

"Old age isn't so bad when you consider the alternative."
—Maurice Chevalier

"Getting old ain't for sissies."
—Bette Davis

"Of late I appear
To have reached that stage
When people look old
Who are only my age."
—Richard Armour

"When I was younger, I could remember anything,
whether it happened or not."
—Mark Twain

"I'm at an age when my back goes out more than I do."
—Phyllis Diller

"You are only young once,
but you can be immature for a lifetime."
—John P. Grier

"If I'd known I was going to live this long (100 years),
I'd have taken better care of myself."
—Ubie Blake

"At twenty years of age the will reigns; at thirty the wit;
and at 40 the judgment."
—Ben Franklin

Vote of Thanks

Here's a simple formula for giving a vote of thanks:

Conclude—give one sentence to indicate that the program is over, and how memorable/meaningful/interesting it has been.

Special Thanks in this order (MMOP)

- Main guest, guests of honour, other guests
- Major donors, sponsors etc
- Other helpers such as those who have helped in other small ways such as setting up venue, catering, free publicity, transport, music, logistics etc.
- Participants.

See You Again—on behalf of the organization thank all and express the hope of seeing them again at the next program and that we act on the training or resolutions of this program.

Don't Thank Yurselves—so no thanks to the President, Manager, Our Team Workers or Project Director.

Weddings

Weddings are a veritable smorgasbord of opportunity for toasts and speeches. The goodwill generated by two people plighting their troth guarantees tears mingled with joy.

It is a great honour to be asked to speak at a wedding. For that reason it is worth working through any reservations you might have and focusing on doing the best you can.

By understanding more about what is involved in crafting a speech or toast, the nervousness evaporates and you will actually start looking forward with anticipation to the experience of standing up and speaking.

You'd like to make your words poignant and memorable. You'd like to make everyone laugh, then shed a tear —which is what a really good wedding toast does.

Coming up with those special words is not that hard, but does require some thought and preparation.

Some simple guides

Begin with humour

This is a great trick for loosening up your audience. Having heard that initial laughter it will also put you in a more relaxed and confident state. The humour can come in the form of a joke, a funny story or an amusing anecdote. Work within your comfort zone of delivery. If you're not a stand-up comedian by profession or someone who has an easy wit, now is not the time to leap into that abyss.

Be sincere

First and foremost, your words must come from the heart. Choose words, thoughts, memories and sentiments that truly reflect how you feel about the person/s you are toasting. Don't try to be what you are not. If your words come from the heart, they will shine like a beacon and stir everyone present.

Share some personal history

After the humorous opening, you can talk about your connection with the person/s you are toasting. It's a great opportunity to give a context and the reason why the honour of toasting this occasion is so meaningful for you—anecdotes to choose can range from the adventurous, funny or poignant experiences you've shared together. Choose a story which will give the audience an indication of the esteem and affection you hold for the person you are toasting.

Don't steal the spotlight

Bear in mind the toast is intended to throw the spotlight upon the subject of the toast, not the toast giver. So make sure the focus for your remarks are firmly on the subject and not yourself.

Balanced delivery

A mistake made by many a best man is to focus only on his mate, the groom. By giving equal time to both, your best mate will think you really are the 'best man' and cement your friendship with his spouse as well.

Short and sweet

You want to hold everyone's attention and deliver the maximum enjoyment for the minimum amount of time. Unless you really are someone very used to holding the audience as a gifted orator, then it's best to keep it brief and heartfelt.

Things to avoid

- **Being overapologetic** "I don't know why I was picked to give a speech...never spoken before in my life..."
- **Being negative or too revealing** "I'm not good at speeches so I'm not going to bore you" or "I went out with Babs for several years before she met Harry..."
- An **extremely brief** response "Thank you"
- **Depressing** "Honoured guests the one person missing here today, is Bab's father—who died only three years ago—and how can any of us ever be really happy in his absence?"
- **Grudging father-in-law** "When we first met Harry neither of us warmed to him very much. When we found out he wanted to marry our daughter..."
- **Gushing** " I am deeply grateful for being asked to speak here today. You couldn't find a nicer more charming more suited couple than Babs and Harry. She is so beautiful and he is such a fine man..."
- **Long and pompous** "Parents of the bride and groom, honoured guests, those who have come from afar, as a judge, professor and minister I feel as though I am eminently capable of speaking about the holy institution of marriage..."

Order and etiquette of speeches

Father Of The Bride Speech

This is traditionally the first speech and its purpose is to:

- Generally welcome the bridal party and guests.
- To praise the bride's loveliness and show pride in his daughter.
- To welcome the Groom into the family.
- To offer a few words of wit and wisdom to the couple.
- To propose a toast to the Bride and Groom.
- To thank all those who have contributed to making this day happen.
- To introduce the Groom, where there is no Toastmaster.

Suggestions for Father of the Bride

"I haven't lost a daughter. I've gained a second mortgage."

"I'm not losing a daughter. I'm gaining a bathroom."

"You know the honeymoon's over when the groom stops helping his wife with the dishes—
and starts doing them himself."

"I'll never forget my wedding day. You never saw two happier people than—her mother and father."

"A good marriage lasts for years. A bad one just seems to."

"Try praising your wife, even though it frightens her at first."

"On the sea of matrimony you have to expect occasional squalls."

"If I were asked for a simple formula for a happy marriage it would have to be, 'Let the husband always have the last two words in any argument—those words, 'Yes, dear'"

Groom's Speech

The second speech in traditional weddings is the groom's and its purpose is:

- To thank the Bride's parents for allowing him to marry their daughter.
- To show his appreciation for his own parents and the happy years he has enjoyed as their son.
- To thank whoever is hosting the wedding and acknowledge those who have contributed to the organization of the wedding.
- To say a few heartfelt things about his new Bride.
- To propose a toast to the Bridesmaids.
- To thank the Best Man, Ushers and Groomsmen.
- A thanks to everyone for the well wishes, cards and presents.
- To introduce the Best Man, if no Toastmaster.

Suggestions For The Groom

"It takes two women to make a good husband—
and the first is his mother."

"I can't imagine a happier way to start married life than with our family and friends around us."

"They say a girl grows to be like her mother—
well I can only hope that's true."

"I want to thank XXXX for agreeing to be Best Man but I'm still a little cautious because I haven't heard his speech yet."

"These charming young ladies have done a great job helping the Bride up the aisle, I just hope that she got to the church of her own free will."

"I don't deserve the good things that have been said about me —but I will try to deserve them and be worthy of my lovely wife."

Best Man's Speech

The third speech falls to the Best Man, and its purpose is:

- To say a few nice things about the Bride and Groom and wish them the best for the future.
- To thank the Groom for choosing him as Best Man.
- To offer a few amusing anecdotes about the Groom, but nothing tasteless or relating to past girlfriends.
- To praise the Bride's appearance and say a few nice things about her.
- To thank the Bride on behalf of the Bridesmaids, and other members of the Bridal party.
- To read out select messages from a few absent friends or relatives.
- To introduce the next agenda item, in the absence of a toastmaster. This could be the cutting of the cake, but must be pre-arranged.

Suggestions For The Best Man

"Ladies and gentlemen, as Henry VIII said to each of his wives, 'I shan't keep you long'."

"There is absolutely nothing wrong with (Groom's name) that a miracle can't fix."

"In all the years I've known him no-one has ever questioned his intelligence. In fact no-one's even mentioned it."

"The trouble with being best man at a wedding is you never get a chance to prove it."

Toasts

To the bride and groom

"The man or woman you really love
Will never grow old to you.
Through the joy and the tears
Through the wrinkles of years
Mutual love will keep shining through!"

"Here's to the bride and the bridegroom,
We'll ask their success in our prayers,
And through life's dark shadows and sunshine
That good luck may always be theirs."

"May the most you wish for be the least you get."

"May you wake up every morning
In each others arms
And count your blessings."

To the two secrets to a long-lasting happy marriage:
Here's to good sense of humour
—and a short memory!

"My Greatest wish for the two of you is that through the years your love for each other will so deepen and grow, that years from now you will look back on this day, your wedding day, as the day you loved each other the least."

"A toast to love and laughter and happy ever after."

"Here's to marriage, that happy estate that resembles a pair of scissors: So joined that they cannot be separated,
often moving in opposite directions,
yet punishing anyone who comes between them."

"Here's to the groom with bride so fair
Here's to the bride with a groom so rare."

"May we all be invited to your golden wedding celebrations."

"Here's to matrimony, the high sea for which
no compass has yet been invented."

"Here's to the groom with bride so fair
Here's to the bride with a groom so rare."

"If you cheat may you cheat death.
If you steal may you steal one another's hearts.
If you fight may you fight for one another.
And if you drink may you drink with me."

"May their joys be deep as the ocean
Their worries as light as the foam."

"Long life, deep love."

"A good wife and health
Are a man's best wealth."

From the bride and groom

"To our best friends,
who know the most about us,
but refuse to believe it."

"May our children be blessed with rich parents."

To the Bride

"To my lovely wife,
The sight of you is as necessary
to me as the sun is to spring."

"May you share everything with your husband,
including the housework."

To the Groom

"To the man who has conquered the bride's heart,
and her mother's."

"Here's to the groom,
a man who keeps his head though he loses his heart."

To the Bridesmaids

"We admire them for their beauty,
respect them for their intelligence,
adore them for their virtues,
and love them because we can't help it."

"To every lovely lady bright,
I wish a gallant faithful knight
To every faithful lover too,
I wish a trusting lady true."

"Here's to our beautiful bridesmaids
A thing of beauty is a joy forever."

"I drink to the general joy of the whole table."

"Here's to women:
they are the loveliest flowers that bloom."

Between the Bride and Groom

"Here's to the woman who knows
all about me and loves me anyway!"

"I have known many,
Liked not a few,
Loved only one
I toast to you."

"Wherever I roam, whatever realms I see,
My heart unravelled fondly turns to thee."
—Oliver Goldsmith

"The world is happy and colourful,
And life itself is new.
And I am very grateful for
The friend I found in you.

To the wings of love:
May they never lose a feather,
But soar up to the sky above,
And last and last forever."

"Every day you look lovelier and lovelier,
and today you look like tomorrow."

"Drink to me only with thine eyes,
And I will pledge with mine;
Or leave a kiss within the cup,
And I'll not look for wine."
—Ben Johnson

"Grow old with me!
The best is yet to be,
The last of life,
For which, the first is made."
—Robert Browning

"Because I love you truly,
Because you love me, too,
My very greatest happiness
Is sharing life with you."

"Were't the last drop in the well,
An I gasp'd upon the brink,
Ere my fainting spirit fell,
'Tis to thee that I would drink.'" —Lord Byron

"Here's to the woman that's good and sweet,
Here's to the woman that's true,
Here's to the woman that rules my heart,
In other words, here's to you."

"Here's to the prettiest, here's to the wittiest,
Here's to the truest of all who are true,
Here's to the neatest one, here's to the sweetest one,
Here's to them, all in one—here's to you."

"To my bride: the woman who makes my life complete."

"I love you more than yesterday and less than tomorrow."

"To the wings of love:
May they never lose a feather,
But soar up to the sky above,
And last and last forever."

"Never above you. Never below you. Always beside you."

"Drink to me only with thine eyes,
And I will pledge with mine;
Or leave a kiss within the cup,
And I'll not look for wine."
—By Ben Jonson

"Today I have married my best friend."

"Merry met, and merry part,
I drink to thee with all my heart."

"Here's looking at you, sweetheart
Though a sea of wine I could pour
My eyes would always thirst for more."

"Here's to my mother-in-law's daughter
Here's to my father-in-law's son
And here's to the vows we've just taken
And the life we've just begun."

From the Parents

"It is written: when children find true love, parents find true joy.
Here's to your joy and ours, from this day forward.
We toast to you!"

"To our dear children on this their special day.
May we grow to know you more and love you more
as time goes by,
share in your joys, and halve your cares. "

Wedding quotes

"There is nothing nobler or more admirable than when two people who see eye-to-eye keep house as man and wife, confounding their enemies and delighting their friends."
—Homer, *The Odyssey*, ninth century BC

"Everything which is exchanged between husband and wife in marriage is the free gift of love. It can never be demanded by one or other as a right."
—Ellen Key

"You don't marry someone you can live with, you marry the person who you cannot live without."
—Author Unknown

"There's only one way to have a happy marriage and as soon as I learn what it is I'll get married again."
—Clint Eastwood

"Happiness is not having what you want, but wanting what you have" —Rabbi H. Schachtel

"The conception of two people living together for twenty-five
years without having a cross word suggests
a lack of spirit only to be admired in sheep."
—Alan Patrick Herbert

"A part of you has grown in me. And so you see, it's you and me
together forever and never apart, maybe in distance,
but never in heart."
—Author Unknown

"The great secret of successful marriage is to treat all disasters as
incidents and none of the incidents as disasters."
—Sir Harold George Nicolson

"Keep your eyes wide open before marriage,
half shut afterwards." —Benjamin Franklin

"Marriage — as its veterans know well—is the continuous
process of getting used to things you hadn't expected."
—Tom Mullen

"A happy marriage is the union of two good forgivers."

Welcome address

Always stand when you are giving the welcoming address. Follow these steps when welcoming the group:

Mr Chairman	Chief guest Mr ...., guest of honour Mr ...., other dignitaries, guests and invitees, press and TV, delegates, participants, ladies and gentlemen.
General welcome	Welcome to the ....(exact name of the program, organised by/hosted by, conducted by ....(Name of organisation)
Organisation	Give two sentences about the organisation.
Occasion	A few sentences about the significance of the program.
Special	Welcome one by one, in only a few sentences in the same order as "Mr" ie chief guest, guest of honour, invitees, press and the people.
End	Again, welcome everybody, hoping that...it would be very useful, reach new heights, be memorable, a turning point, a milestone, create history...

Overcoming the Fear of Speaking in Public

Public speaking is the most common social phobia and can be a significant problem if one's work or study requires participation in group discussions and/or the giving of presentations.

It is believed to be the single most common phobia, affecting as much as 75% of all people. When ranked among fears, it generally is the number one fear, on par with fear of dying.

Here are some helpful directives which will help you overcome that fear and help to make it something you look forward to:

•**Volunteer** for speaking opportunities—start small but practice often. It's the best way to build confidence. Join a speaking group such as Toastmasters or Rostrum - this is a non-threatening, enjoyable way first to overcome fear, then to build skill and competence in public speaking.

•**Accept** selectively on areas you are familiar with and have sufficient time to prepare for. Otherwise tell them politely NO. Even though it can be very good to explore new ground, as a beginner it is foolish. You need to be concentrating on delivery not the subject matter.

•**Prepare** before you get there, but never prepare, worry or think about it once you're there. Make what you say short and sweet and to the point.

•**Arrive early** at the venue and familiarise yourself with the hall, dais, podium, microphone, organisers, staff and amenities.

•**Greet** the people, introduce yourself, smile at strangers, laugh, smile and generally cheer up. This really helps to get you in a state of can-do.

•**Relax** both mentally and physically while you are waiting your turn to speak. Take deep breaths, make a mini-meditation, indulge in some positive self-talk, feel your friends around you giving support, and remember past successes. Then give your full attention to what is happening in the spotlight.

•**Rise slowly** when your name is called, walk in a normal pace to the dais, climb up, look at the people, smile and assume your stance.